LEVEL 1

SCIENCE

LET'S READ AND FIND OUT

WHAT'S FOR LUNCH?

SARAH L. THOMSON · ILLUSTRATED BY NILA AYE

HARPER

An Imprint of HarperCollinsPublishers

Special thanks to Dr. Carolyn Johnson, PhD, FAAHB, NCC, LPA, Director of the Tulane Prevention Research Center, and Keelia O'Malley, MPH, Assistant Director of the Prevention Research Center at Tulane University, for their valuable assistance.

The Let's-Read-and-Find-Out Science book series was originated by Dr. Franklyn M. Branley, Astronomer Emeritus and former Chairman of the American Museum of Natural History–Hayden Planetarium, and was formerly co-edited by him and Dr. Roma Gans, Professor Emeritus of Childhood Education, Teachers College, Columbia University. Text and illustrations for each of the books in the series are checked for accuracy by an expert in the relevant field. For more information about Let's-Read-and-Find-Out Science books, write to HarperCollins Children's Books, 195 Broadway, New York, NY 10007, or visit our website at www.letsreadandfindout.com.

Library of Congress Control Number: 2015940705
ISBN 978-0-06-233138-0 (trade bdg.)—ISBN 978-0-06-233137-3 (pbk.)

The artist used her imagination and Adobe Illustrator CS6 to create the digital illustrations for this book.
Typography by Erica De Chavez
15 16 17 18 19   SCP   10 9 8 7 6 5 4 3 2 1
❖
First Edition

For Tamar—S.T.

To my children, Lili and Tom, who are an ongoing
source of inspiration and laughter to me—N.A.

My tummy is empty. It's even making a growling noise. I'm hungry! What's for lunch?

A turkey sandwich. Crunchy carrots. A glass of
milk. And a chocolate-covered strawberry for dessert.

10

Can I just eat chocolate-covered
strawberries for lunch? Mom says no.
Dad says no.

Why not?

Mom says my body needs different things to eat. Dad says each kind of food on my plate does a job.

PROTEIN

tofu

eggs

nuts

meat

peanut butter

seeds

fish

cheese

beans

milk

My turkey has **protein**. So does my milk. Protein builds my muscles and bones so that they stay strong and I can grow.

My bread has **carbohydrates** to fill me up with quick energy.

CARBOHYDRATES

bread

rice

pasta

granola bar

oatmeal

corn

popcorn

cereal

My chocolate has **fat**. Fat can give me a lot of energy! Plus, my body uses it to store vitamins and to build all sorts of things.

My body saves up fat for when I need it,
and it can keep fat inside me for a long time.
So I need to eat only a little bit at a time.

My strawberries have **vitamin C**. My carrots have **vitamin A**. My body needs a lot of different vitamins, and each one has its own job.

VITAMINS

Vitamin A is good for skin, hair, and eyes.

carrot | sweet potato | cantaloupe

Vitamin C helps the body heal itself.

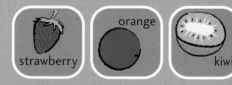

strawberry | orange | kiwi

My strawberries and my carrots have **fiber** too. So does my whole-wheat bread. Fiber helps my body get rid of waste—stuff it doesn't need inside.

Vitamin D is good for bones and teeth. We get it from food but also from sunlight.

Vitamin E helps keep you healthy.

Vitamin K is good for bones and helps blood clot after a cut.

My milk has a **mineral** called calcium. Calcium makes my teeth and bones strong. Other foods have other minerals that my body needs.

My milk has **water** too. Water keeps my body from getting too hot or too cold, and it helps wash out waste. I need to drink a lot of water to stay healthy!

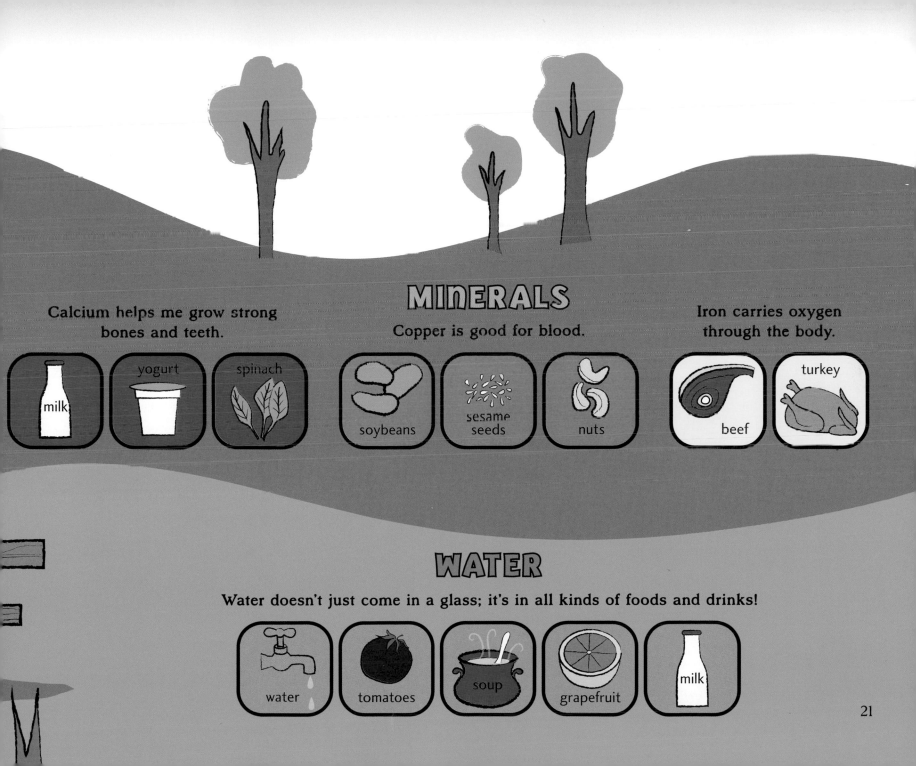

MINERALS

Calcium helps me grow strong
bones and teeth.

milk

yogurt

spinach

Copper is good for blood.

soybeans

sesame
seeds

nuts

Iron carries oxygen
through the body.

beef

turkey

WATER

Water doesn't just come in a glass; it's in all kinds of foods and drinks!

water

tomatoes

soup

grapefruit

milk

21

Some food does only one job for my body.
Sugar has **carbohydrates** and nothing else. That
gives me quick energy, but it doesn't last long.

Foods that are better for me do a lot of jobs at once. A peanut butter sandwich on whole-wheat bread has . . .

protein (for bones and muscles) AND
carbohydrates (for energy) AND
fat (for even more energy) AND
fiber (to help get rid of waste) AND
vitamins and minerals (to make my body work right).

Food builds bones and muscles.
It helps me grow.
It gets rid of waste.
It keeps me healthy.
And it does a lot more!

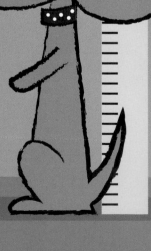

Most of all, food gives me energy.
I couldn't play or talk or think or even
breathe without energy.

The energy in food is measured in **calories**.
All foods have calories. How many I get depends
on what foods I pick and how much I eat.

To get one hundred calories of energy, I could eat:

1 scrambled egg OR
2 thin slices of ham OR
1 cup of grapes OR
2 cups of cherry tomatoes OR
½ cup of noodles with butter OR
½ plain bagel OR
1 small piece of chocolate.

There's an easy way to make sure I'm getting what my body needs. I can split up my plate into four parts.

FRUITS

One part is for **fruit**—like my strawberry.

VEGETABLES

One part is for **vegetables**—like my carrots.

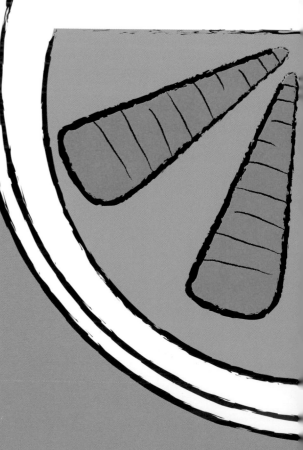

One part is for **carbohydrates**—like the bread in my sandwich.

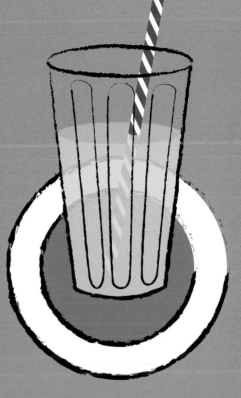

Plus I can fill up a glass with milk or water.

PROTEIN

One part is for **protein**—like my turkey.

I can kick a ball in soccer. I can do a cartwheel. I can figure out a problem. I can color a picture. I can grow and grow and *grow*!

31

But I can't do any of
these things without food.
Time for lunch!

32

GLOSSARY

Calorie: A way to measure energy

Carbohydrates (People say "carbs" for short.): Something in food that gives the body quick energy. Bread, rice, and pasta all contain lots of carbohydrates.

Fat: Something in food that gives the body long-lasting energy. Butter, cream, and oil all have lots of fat.

Fiber: Parts of food, such as the skin of an apple, that the body cannot use. Fiber passes through the body and helps clear out other waste.

Fruit: Food that contains the seeds of a plant

Mineral: Something our bodies need but cannot make for themselves and that did not come from a living source. Minerals can be rocks (like calcium) or metals (like iron).

Protein: Something in food that builds muscles and bones. Eggs, meat, and beans have protein.

Vegetable: Food that comes from a plant. A vegetable can be a leaf (spinach), a flower (broccoli), a root (carrot), or a seed (pea).

Vitamin: Something our bodies need but cannot make for themselves and that comes from plants or animals. (There is one vitamin our bodies can make directly from sunlight—vitamin D. But we can also get vitamin D from food.)

Eat a RAINBOW!

Many of the vitamins that our bodies need come from fruits and vegetables. One way to be sure you are getting all the vitamins you need is to eat fruits and vegetables that are different colors.

Take a look at your plate. Is your food mostly white? Try adding something colorful—some orange cantaloupe, a purple grape, a green string bean.

You can also make a rainbow chart, like this:

Day 1						
Day 2						
Day 3						
Day 4						

Each day, make a dot or a check mark to show how many red, orange, yellow, green, blue, or purple things you ate. How many days does take it take you to eat a whole rainbow?

Teaching your children or students about nutrition at an early age can create lifelong healthy eating habits. This book is a great starting point for kids to learn to make smart food choices, but there are a few additional thoughts I'd like to share with you as an adult.

As the book says, while fat is an important part of a healthy diet, we don't need to eat a lot of it because our bodies store and use fat as fuel for a long time. Not all fats are created equal; make sure your kids get most of the fat in their diets from "good," or unsaturated, fats like those found in plant foods and fish. I also recommend that when choosing foods that have a high fat content, like milk, go for a low-fat version. Kids will still get the flavor of the food but with less fat and fewer calories.

My other important piece of advice is to encourage kids to drink lots of water, especially at mealtimes. Many soft drinks, juices, and other sugar-sweetened beverages contain high levels of sugar and calories. Teaching kids to drink plenty of water is an important health behavior that will last a lifetime!

Happy eating!

Carolyn C. Johnson

PhD, FAAHB, NCC, LPA
Usdin Family Professor
Director, Tulane Prevention Research Center
Tulane University School of Public Health & Tropical Medicine

This book meets the Common Core State Standards
for Science and Technical Subjects. For Common Core
resources for this title and others, please visit
www.readcommoncore.com.

Be sure to look for all of these books in the Let's-Read-and-Find-Out Science series: